Original title:
A Silent Chill

Copyright © 2024 Swan Charm
All rights reserved.

Author: Aron Pilviste
ISBN HARDBACK: 978-9916-79-729-7
ISBN PAPERBACK: 978-9916-79-730-3
ISBN EBOOK: 978-9916-79-731-0

# **Frostbitten Reveries**

In the hush of winter's breath,
Dreams whisper softly, nothing left.
Snowflakes dance on silent ground,
Echoes of peace in chill profound.

Midnight skies adorned with stars,
A silver glow from Venus far.
Shadows play in twilight's grace,
Memory's warmth in a frozen space.

Footsteps trace the hidden path,
Breath like mist in nature's bath.
Each moment wrapped in crystal clear,
Time suspended, held so dear.

Windsong weaves through barren trees,
Nature's song, a gentle breeze.
Every flake a tale untold,
Whispers of warmth in the bitter cold.

Eyes alight with frosted dreams,
Life unfolds in silver beams.
In this realm where dreams take flight,
Frostbitten wonders dance in night.

## Echoes of the Icy Expanse


Across the tundra, whispers call,
Traces of winter's quiet thrall.
Endless white 'neath pale blue skies,
Nature's canvas, calm and wise.

Footprints lost, then found again,
Marking journeys through the plain.
Every breath, a spark in frost,
Echoes linger, never lost.

Glaciers creak, and silence reigns,
Frozen lakes, untouched by chains.
Underneath lies a world unseen,
Where secrets dwell, and dreams convene.

Shadows stretch as daylight fades,
Whirling snow in veils cascades.
A symphony of winter's might,
Playing soft in the fading light.

In this land where echoes roam,
Peaceful heart can find a home.
Echoes whisper, softly sway,
In the icy expanse, we stay.

## **Twilight on the Frozen Lake**

Twilight sings on glassy shores,
Crimson skies, and nature soars.
Underneath, the waters dream,
A tranquil pulse, a muted gleam.

Silence deep, as shadows dance,
The world held in a fleeting glance.
Feet can glide on winter's skin,
In this realm where joy begins.

Frost-kissed reeds in stillness sway,
Night's embrace whispers, 'Come and play.'
Magic woven in the air,
Moments linger, soft and rare.

Veiled in hues of blue and grey,
Nature's breath leads dreams astray.
Stars ignite, and hearts ignite,
Under the cloak of snowy night.

In the twilight's tender light,
Frozen visions take their flight.
Each heartbeat blends with winter's song,
In this stillness, we belong.

## Sighs of an Unyielding Night

Beneath the sky, the cold winds sigh,
Stars shimmer, whispering goodbye.
Night enfolds in velvet gloom,
Embracing all in icy bloom.

Frostbitten dreams weave through the air,
Moments frozen, nothing to compare.
The world, a canvas pale and stark,
Breathless nights in the lingering dark.

Moonlight spills like silver threads,
Lighting paths where silence spreads.
In the shadows, secrets weave,
Promises only night can conceive.

Echoes call from woods so deep,
Cocooned in quiet, nature sleeps.
Heartbeats quicken 'neath the skies,
Sighs of life as stillness lies.

Stars bear witness to the plight,
In the sorrow of an unyielding night.
Frozen memories drift away,
Holding tight to dreams that sway.

## **Hibernation's Quiet Dream**

In the silence, shadows creep,
While the world is fast asleep.
Whispers of a tale unfold,
Wrapped in dreams, both soft and bold.

Beneath the blanket, earth does sigh,
Hidden depths where secrets lie.
Time slows down, a gentle pause,
Nature rests without a cause.

Snowflakes dance in silver light,
Painting stars that shine so bright.
Every branch adorned with white,
Echoes of the tranquil night.

Fires crackle, embers glow,
Stories shared in whispers low.
As we nestle, hearts entwine,
In this dream, we find the divine.

Spring will come, the cycle turns,
Yet in this warmth, the spirit yearns.
For hibernation's quiet grace,
Carries a soft, enduring trace.

## **Whispers of Winter's Breath**

A breath of frost upon the air,
Winter comes with a gentle stare.
Silent nights wrapped in blue,
Stars emerge, a stunning view.

Trees stand tall in purest white,
Guardians of the crystal night.
Whispers carried on the breeze,
Nature's secrets, hearts at ease.

Footprints crunch on frozen ground,
Echoes of life's beauty found.
In the stillness, magic weaves,
Tales of wonder, love achieves.

Warmth within, though cold outside,
Hope ignites like a glowing tide.
Moments shared by candle's glow,
In winter's grasp, our spirits flow.

When the world lies still and bare,
In the quiet, hearts repair.
Whispers of a season's grace,
Winter's breath, a warm embrace.

## Echoes in the Frost

Footsteps soft in powdery snow,
Echoes linger where few dare go.
In the chill, a silent song,
Nature's voice, soft yet strong.

Breath like smoke in frigid air,
Delicate flakes dance without care.
The moonlight bathes the world in glow,
Casting shadows, bright and low.

Branches bow with heavy load,
Silent whispers on the road.
Echoes drift through frosty trees,
Carried gently by the breeze.

By the fire, warmth draws near,
Stories shared, laughter clear.
In the hearth, the heart ignites,
With the beauty of these nights.

When morning breaks in softest light,
Frosted dreams take their flight.
Echoes linger, sweet and near,
In the season we hold dear.

## The Quiet of December Nights

December wraps us in its fold,
A tapestry of stories told.
Stars like whispers in the sky,
In the silence, souls comply.

Wrapped in blankets, hearts entwine,
Hot cocoa sips, a taste so fine.
Outside, the world dressed in white,
Inside, warmth against the night.

Candles flicker, shadows dance,
In this stillness, we find our chance.
To reflect on days gone by,
Underneath the winter sky.

Moments shared in whispered tones,
In this quiet, we're not alone.
The night holds peace, a calming balm,
In the chill, we find the warm.

As December wears her crown,
We find beauty all around.
In the quiet of these nights,
Peace and joy take gentle flights.

## **The Grasp of the Frigid Night**

Stars twinkle like diamonds bright,
The chill whispers secrets tight.
Trees stand tall with frosted breath,
In the stillness, dreams take death.

Moonlight spills on icy ground,
In the silence, a haunting sound.
Shadows dance on frosty air,
Wrapped in the night's deep despair.

Footsteps crunch on snowy trails,
Echoing where the cold prevails.
Hearts beat strong against the freeze,
In this moment, time must seize.

Distant howls of midnight's wail,
Tales of love and frozen frail.
Yet in darkness, warmth can start,
From the grasp, we won't depart.

Breathe the wintry essence deep,
In this night, our secrets keep.
Through the cold, a fire ignites,
In the grasp of frigid nights.

## Subdued Shadows in the Cold

In the twilight, shadows loom,
Their whispers weave a silent gloom.
Colors fade, the day retreats,
Embracing winter's calm defeats.

Branches bare against the sky,
Witness stillness as time flies by.
Footfalls trace on gleaming snow,
Silent secrets of hearts that glow.

A flicker of warmth in the air,
Hints of memories linger there.
Subdued echoes of laughter ring,
In this cold, what joy can bring?

Solitude drapes like a veil,
Each breath tells a chilling tale.
Yet within this frozen night,
Hope flickers, buddings of light.

Under starlit blankets wide,
We find comfort in the quiet side.
Subdued shadows in the cold,
Embrace the stories yet untold.

## Memories Engulfed in Ice

Frozen moments drift away,
Each memory, a price to pay.
Captured in a glittering glaze,
Lost in the winter's icy maze.

Time stands still in the frost's embrace,
Echoes of laughter find their place.
Fleeting glimpses of days gone by,
Beneath the vast and starry sky.

Whispers of warmth in the freeze,
Soft and gentle, like winter trees.
Embers glow beneath the chill,
In the heart, a longing thrill.

Grasping fragments of what has been,
In the silence, memories glean.
Engulfed by ice, yet not alone,
In this cold, our essence shone.

Each flake a tale, a whisper shared,
In the quiet, souls are bared.
Memories adrift, so precise,
Forever held in winter's ice.

## **The Fragile Quiet of Winter's Hold**

Snowflakes fall with tender grace,
Covering earth in a pale embrace.
The world slows, a breath that's deep,
In winter's hold, secrets we keep.

A blanket softens every sound,
In this stillness, peace is found.
Moments linger, time takes pause,
In the quiet, nature's laws.

Frosty whispers brush the trees,
Nature sighs in the biting breeze.
Yet within this chill, hearts warm,
Finding solace in the storm.

Underneath the frozen skies,
Dreams awaken, hopes arise.
Even in the coldest breath,
Life persists beyond the death.

Fragile quiet blankets all,
As shadows dance in subtle thrall.
In winter's grasp, we find our way,
Through the night into the day.

## Secrets beneath the Snowdrift

Beneath the soft, white blanket, lies
Stories hidden from the eyes,
Whispers of what used to be,
Frozen memories, wild and free.

Each flake a tale, unique and bright,
Dancing down in silent flight,
Nature's secrets softly kept,
In the drifts where winter swept.

Footprints lost in the deep maze,
Mark the wanderers' quiet praise,
Of hidden worlds covered tight,
In the glow of pale twilight.

Branches bow with weighted grace,
Crystals shimmer, nature's lace,
In this realm, the stillness sings,
Of the wonders that winter brings.

When spring breathes warm upon the land,
These secrets rise, dusted and fanned,
Yet for now, they softly wait,
Beneath the snow, sealed in fate.

## Solitude in the Shivering Air

Alone I walk through barren trees,
A chilling breeze that bends the knees,
Each breath a cloud of ice and fog,
In the silence, I find my cog.

Footsteps echo on the ground,
A solitary, haunting sound,
Whispers ride the frosty trail,
In solitude, my thoughts set sail.

The scent of pine, crisp and clear,
Wraps around, draws me near,
To the heart of winter's dream,
Where even shadows softly gleam.

Sky painted gray, a muted hue,
Yet within, a warmth imbues,
In the cold, I find my peace,
In solitude, my soul's release.

As twilight falls, stars peek shy,
A diamond dust against the sky,
In the shivering air I stand,
Embracing all that's winter's hand.

## Ghostly Murmurs of the Glacial Past

Echoes rise from icy streams,
Whispers float on silver beams,
Stories carved in ancient ice,
Time entwined with every slice.

The glaciers shift, a solemn dance,
To the rhythm of nature's chance,
Carving valleys deep and wide,
In stillness, where the secrets hide.

Frozen tears of ages old,
Tales of warmth, now icy cold,
In the silence, voices cling,
Of histories and what they bring.

The land remembers every sigh,
Underneath a pale blue sky,
And every crack that echoes loud,
Together, form a ghostly shroud.

The past unfolds in layers thin,
As time recedes, and dreams begin,
In glacial arms, the world does rest,
Whispers of what we've all suppressed.

## The Calm before the Storm

Beneath the sky, a breathless hush,
The world awaits the thunder's rush,
Stillness holds the distant cries,
In the heart, anticipation lies.

Clouds gather, dark and deep,
Nature lingers, starts to creep,
The air electric, thick with fate,
In this pause, we contemplate.

Birds retreat, the trees stand tall,
Nature braces for the call,
In the calm, secrets unveil,
As the winds begin to sail.

Lightning flickers, a fleeting spark,
Promises flicker in the dark,
Yet in this moment, time stands still,
A gentle whisper of nature's will.

And when the storm breaks free at last,
It's a symphony, unsurpassed,
But until then, we hold our breath,
The calm before the dance of death.

## The Secret of Stillness

In the hush of the twilight glow,
Whispers weave where shadows grow.
Silent heartbeats, breathless sighs,
Time stands still beneath the skies.

Nature holds her secrets tight,
In the velvet cloak of night.
Every rustle, every breeze,
Brings a calm that softly frees.

Thoughts drift gently, like the leaves,
Carried on the night's soft eves.
In this pause, we find our grace,
In the stillness, we embrace.

Stars above, a guiding light,
Watching o'er our dreams take flight.
In the quiet, truths unfold,
Whispers of the soul retold.

Beneath the moon's serene expanse,
Life awaits a second chance.
In the still, we learn to see,
The sacred art of simply be.

## Murmurs of a Slumbering World

In the cradle of twilight's hue,
Softly sighs the world anew.
Mountains whisper, valleys hum,
Nature's heart beats, calm and numb.

Stars awaken, twinkling bright,
Guiding dreams through softest night.
Each rustle tells a tale unheard,
In the silence, life is stirred.

Waves caress the sleeping shore,
Muffled echoes, ancient lore.
In the darkness, shadows dance,
Every heart beats in a trance.

Crickets serenade the air,
Nature's song is rich and rare.
As the world wraps in its sleep,
Secrets of the night we keep.

Morning waits with yawning skies,
Yet in slumber, magic lies.
In the stillness, all unfurls,
Murmurs of a slumbering world.

## **Frost's Soft Caress**

Morning dawns with silver grace,
Frosty whispers lace the place.
Natures blanket, crisp and clear,
Hides the warmth and draws us near.

In the chill, a breathless light,
Sparkles dance, a dazzling sight.
Every branch, a crystal throne,
Nature's beauty fully grown.

Footsteps crunch on icy ground,
Symphonies of frost abound.
Frozen blooms in quiet awe,
Capturing the world we saw.

Winter's kiss, so soft, so sweet,
Nature's heart slows down its beat.
In this season, life's embrace,
Finds a warmth in frost's soft grace.

As the sun begins to rise,
Glistening under azure skies,
Frost will fade, yet in its place,
Memories of its soft embrace.

## The Last Leaf's Farewell

In the chill of autumn's sigh,
One last leaf drifts from the sky.
Crimson whispers as it falls,
Nature's voice in hushed calls.

Lingering on a branch so frail,
It dances boldly without fail.
Golden hues and twilight blend,
Marking time as seasons end.

The breeze carries its tale aloft,
A testament, both sad and soft.
Amidst the branches, memories cling,
Of all the warmth that fall can bring.

Nature stands as time extends,
As every journey slowly bends.
The last leaf knows its time to leave,
In the silence, we will grieve.

With a flutter, it meets the ground,
In its stillness, peace is found.
Nature whispers a sweet farewell,
To the last leaf, stories to tell.

## Ethereal Glimmers Amidst the Chill

Ghostly whispers fill the air,
Stars twinkle with a gentle glare.
Moonlight dances on frozen streams,
Awakening the world from dreams.

Shadows flicker in the night,
Casting shapes that feel just right.
Breath mists like clouds in dusk,
Ensconced in winter's frosty husk.

Breathless beauty all around,
In quiet corners, magic found.
Silver dust drapes every tree,
A tapestry of chill so free.

Ethereal moments, fleeting grace,
Nature's charm in cold embrace.
With each step, the world awakes,
In our hearts, the silence shakes.

Stars fade in the morning's light,
Echoes of the frosty night.
We carry glimmers from the chill,
A warmth that whispers, stay until.

## **Blue Hues of an Untold Winter**

Shades of blue in crisp dawn air,
Whispers of frost, beyond compare.
Horizon painted with icy tint,
Nature's palette, cold and glint.

Frozen lakes like glass reflect,
Every secret we dare protect.
Beneath the snow, life still stirs,
In hidden realms, the heartbeat purrs.

Winds carry tales of past delight,
A symphony of winter's bite.
Footprints trace a path anew,
In the hush of morning's blue.

Icicles hang like crystal chimes,
Marking moments, timeless rhymes.
Echoes of silence, soft and pure,
In the stillness, we endure.

A season draped in tranquil hues,
Tales untold, a world to cruise.
With each breath, a story spins,
In the blue, where winter begins.

## The Mysteries in Frosted Silence

In the stillness, questions bloom,
Veiled in whispers, secrets loom.
Frosty patterns on windowpanes,
Tell the tales of winter's reign.

Silent echoes, shadows creep,
Through the woods, where dreamers sleep.
Every flake, a story spun,
Holding wonders, one by one.

Amidst the chill, a hush prevails,
Nature weaves her silent tales.
Footsteps muffled, hearts aligned,
In frosted silence, peace we find.

Branches laden with silver lace,
A quiet reverie, time and space.
Beneath the snow, the earth will weave,
Life's mysteries we can't perceive.

Dancing shadows, fleeting light,
In the depth of winter's night.
Listen closely to the hush,
For in silence, dreams still rush.

## **Frigid Whispers**

In the chill of night, secrets sigh,
Where shadows dance beneath the sky.
Soft murmurs echo in the snow,
Silent tales that only frost can know.

Stars twinkle like icy tears,
A tapestry woven through the years.
Each breath a cloud in the freezing air,
Ethereal whispers linger everywhere.

Branches creak under frost's grip,
Nature holds its frozen lip.
A world wrapped in silence deep,
As winter secrets softly creep.

Moonlight bathes the frosty ground,
In its glow, lost dreams are found.
Frigid whispers, cold yet clear,
Call to hearts that long to hear.

Through the stillness, spirits roam,
Searching for a place called home.
In the night where shadows play,
Frigid whispers guide the way.

## **Beneath the Crystal Veil**

Underneath a veil of ice,
The world transforms, cold yet nice.
A glimmering landscape, pure and bright,
Wrapped in winter's tender light.

Frozen lakes, a mirror's gleam,
Reflecting all our frozen dreams.
Each step crunches on the ground,
In this beauty, peace is found.

Trees adorned like crystal queens,
Whisper secrets in frost's glean.
Quiet moments breathe like prayer,
Beneath the crystal, magic's air.

The heart finds solace, pure and true,
In the silence, winter's hue.
A hidden realm, both vast and small,
Where nature's wonders call us all.

Beneath the veil, time stands still,
In this embrace, we find our will.
Life's simple joy, a fleeting dance,
In the crystal stillness, we take a chance.

## **Icy Tendrils of Memory**

Fingers of frost lace the windows,
Tracing stories only one knows.
Icy tendrils reach and weave,
Connecting the past, we believe.

Gentle shadows whisper names,
Echoes of laughter, love's sweet games.
In frozen frames, the moments freeze,
Time suspends, offering peace.

Each crack of ice holds a tale,
Of sunlit days and winter's veil.
Lost in thought, we slip away,
Chasing warmth on a silver day.

In the stillness, past and present meet,
As icy tendrils pull at our feet.
Memory dances through the chill,
An unbroken bond that lingers still.

Glistening paths lead us to find,
The heart's connection, intertwined.
In every flake, a story spins,
Icy tendrils, where life begins.

## Lament of the Frostbitten Earth

The land lies still, a frozen sigh,
Underneath the sullen sky.
Shattered dreams in ice confined,
Nature weeps for what's left behind.

Gray clouds gather, heavy with woe,
Covering the seeds that long to grow.
A barren field, stripped of cheer,
Holds the echoes of what was dear.

Frostbitten whispers fill the air,
Reminders of the sun's lost care.
With every gust, a memory fades,
In this silence, beauty invades.

Yet in the chill, hope stirs anew,
Despite the frost, life's essence grew.
The earth may weep, but dreams take flight,
A promise of warmth hidden from sight.

Lament resounds through the frozen trees,
A symphony played on winter's breeze.
For every end, a beginning reigns,
In frostbitten sorrow, life remains.

## **Stillness Wrapped in Crystal**

In the quiet, whispers sigh,
A world adorned in frost's soft light.
Branches gleam, like dreams on high,
Nature holds its breath tonight.

Moonbeams dance on icy lakes,
Stars twinkle in a velvet sea.
Every moment gently quakes,
In stillness, hearts begin to see.

Footfalls muffled, time stands still,
Crisp air wraps around my soul.
A tranquil warmth begins to fill,
This crystal world makes me feel whole.

Snowflakes fall, a quiet grace,
Each one tells a tale untold.
In this serene, enchanted space,
A thousand secrets now unfold.

Boundless beauty, pure and rare,
Nature's canvas, clean and bright.
In this moment, free from care,
I'm wrapped in crystal, pure delight.

# Echoes of the Unseen Chill

Whispers weave through barren trees,
A breath of winter, soft and sly.
Ghostly shadows cling with ease,
As dormant worlds begin to lie.

Crystalline winds brush my face,
Echoes linger, cold and clear.
Each heartbeat finds a hidden place,
In the silence, I draw near.

Footsteps quiet on a path,
Where warmth seems a distant dream.
Life pauses, holding back wrath,
In the chill, emotions gleam.

The moon hangs low, a silver coin,
Illuminating the frost-kissed ground.
In this moment, I feel adjoin,
To the echoes that life has found.

Time bends in this frozen grace,
Every breath a fragile thread.
In shadows where memories trace,
The unseen chill lingers ahead.

# The Calm Before the Flurry

A hush envelops the darkened sky,
As night prepares for morning's show.
Each breath held as dreams drift by,
In the calm, anticipation flows.

Stars shiver in their distant gaze,
The world awaits a soft delight.
Winter's breath in gentle phase,
A lull before the storm ignites.

Frosty silhouettes stand still,
Whispers mingle with the night.
Nature holds a timeless thrill,
In this pause, all feels right.

Moonlight dims, a graceful sway,
As dawn approaches, bright and bold.
In silence, I find my way,
To the stories yet untold.

Awaiting splendor, crisp and clear,
Each moment precious, softly spun.
In this calm, I feel the near,
Of a flurry bound to run.

## **Frostbitten Serenade**

Chill notes played on winter's breath,
A melody of ice and white.
In every sigh, a dance with death,
The world indeed feels cold and bright.

Crystals twinkle, lightly sway,
Like starry thoughts on snowy ground.
In this song, I lose my way,
To the whispers all around.

Nature sings a haunting tune,
With frosty fingers strumming high.
A serenade beneath the moon,
As winter winds begin to sigh.

Every flake a note divine,
Together crafting symphonies.
In this realm, my heart aligns,
With the pulse of frozen trees.

So let the frostbite bring its spell,
In this season, pure and grand.
In the serenade, I dwell,
In the chill, I take my stand.

## **The Solitude of Snowflakes**

In the quiet air they drift,
Whispers soft, a gentle gift.
Dancing down from skies so gray,
Each a memory on display.

Lying still on earth's embrace,
Covering the world with grace.
A soft layer, pure and bright,
Silent beauty, softest light.

Lost in thought, they swirl and spin,
Finding peace where they begin.
No two alike in form or fate,
Each one unique, no room for hate.

Time stands still as they descend,
Nature's art that has no end.
In their fall, we find our chance,
To pause, to dream, to join their dance.

As the world is wrapped in white,
Snowflakes whisper through the night.
In solitude, they softly wait,
For the sun's warm touch, their fate.

## **Glistening Secrets Underfoot**

Beneath the frost, tales unfold,
Of hidden paths and secrets told.
Each crack and crunch, a story brings,
Echoes of forgotten things.

Glistening like diamonds bright,
Nature's wonders, pure delight.
Every step a fleeting sound,
Whispers linger underground.

Shadows dance in morning light,
Footprints fade, out of sight.
Frozen moments can't withstand,
Nature's brush, a master's hand.

What lies beneath this icy sheet?
A world alive, a heart that beats.
Secrets waiting to be found,
In the stillness, truths abound.

As we walk through snow and ice,
We tread on dreams, a step precise.
Glistening secrets, bold and bright,
Whisper softly in the night.

## **Threads of Cold Silence**

In the tapestry of night,
Threads of silence take their flight.
Starlit whispers, shadows fall,
Wrap the world in their soft thrall.

Each breath taken, crisp and loud,
Muffles deep in winter's shroud.
Hushed reflections, icy clear,
Draw us near, dispelling fear.

Through the stillness, echoes creep,
In this beauty, secrets seep.
A moment's pause, a fleeting glance,
In the darkness, we find trance.

Woven in the frosty air,
Memories linger, brave and rare.
Cold surrounds yet feels like home,
In solitude, our minds can roam.

Each quiet thought, a thread we weave,
In the darkness, we believe.
Threads of silence tight and strong,
Guide our hearts where they belong.

## Secrets Beneath the Glaze

Underneath the icy veil,
Lie the stories, soft and frail.
Shattered dreams in winter's hold,
Whispers of the brave and bold.

A shiny coat over the past,
Preserved moments that won't last.
Crystalline layers, pure and fine,
Guard the truths, both yours and mine.

Every crack, a whisper's tale,
Echoes of the winds that wail.
What lies hidden waiting there,
Longing hearts, a silent prayer.

As we walk on slippery paths,
We uncover winter's laughs.
Beneath each glaze, there's more to see,
A universe that longs to be.

Secrets shimmer, soft and bright,
In the stillness of the night.
Underneath the frost's embrace,
Lies a world, a sacred space.

## **The Still Echo of Cold Days**

Beneath the gray and heavy skies,
The whispers of the winter sighs.
Branches bare, their secrets hold,
A story wrapped in tender cold.

The winds they speak in muted tones,
A distant call of chilling moans.
Footprints trace the paths we tread,
Where silent thoughts of warmth are fed.

Frosted fields in quiet repose,
Each blade of grass a trodden prose.
Nature's breath, a still refrain,
In the still echo of cold rain.

The sun a stranger, shy and pale,
Wrapped beneath a winter veil.
Yet in this hush of frigid air,
Lies beauty, stark and rare.

As dusk descends, the world turns white,
A canvas painted soft and light.
With every breath, the cold ingrains,
The beauty found in winter's chains.

## Frigid Fables

Where icy tales in shadows dwell,
The frosty fables weave and swell.
With every flake that gently falls,
A silent truth within it calls.

Stories born of crystal frost,
In whispered dreams, a warmth embossed.
The chilly air, a breath divine,
Crafts the magic of the pine.

Through frozen woods, the night drifts near,
Each step a spark, though hard to steer.
Beneath the boughs that bow so low,
The hidden tales of winters flow.

The moon holds court in skies so clear,
With silver beams that gently cheer.
In every corner, mystique gleams,
An echo of a thousand dreams.

So let the frostbite touch your soul,
For in the chill, we find our whole.
The stories spun in white embrace,
Are frigid fables time can't erase.

## A Dream of White Confusion

In swirling mists of winter's breath,
A dream unfolds of soft, white death.
Each flake a dancer, wild and free,
Whispers of chaos, tender glee.

Through drifting fogs, the vision spins,
With every gust, new tales begins.
This tapestry of snow and light,
Wraps the world in misty white.

Each step we take, a fleeting trace,
In this enigma, we lose our pace.
The ground is lost, horizon bent,
A canvas where no maps are sent.

And in the hush, confusion reigns,
As beauty masks the bitter gains.
We wander through a blurred design,
In every corner, dreams entwine.

So let the snow fall deep and wide,
For in this dream, we must abide.
With hearts aglow in winter's tune,
A dream of white beneath the moon.

## The Hush of Snowfall

The hush of snowfall fills the night,
With whispers soft and pure delight.
Each flake a promise, gently thrown,
On earth's embrace, a silent moan.

Beneath the stars, the world transforms,
In quiet grace, the snow conforms.
It blankets all in peace profound,
A tranquil spell that stirs the ground.

The trees stand still, their branches bare,
Heavy with dreams that float on air.
In nature's pause, the heartbeat slows,
As magic through the stillness flows.

With every flurry, time stands still,
In this embrace, we find our will.
The morning light unveils the scene,
A canvas washed in pure marine.

And as the world awakes anew,
We hear the whispers, soft and true.
In every flake, a story's told,
The hush of snowfall, pure and bold.

## **Subtle Remnants of Cold**

Whispers of frost cling to the night,
Chill that lingers, soft and light.
Breath of winter, fading slow,
Echoes of warmth, in a gentle glow.

Footsteps tread on silent ground,
Nature's hush, a world unbound.
Branches bow with frosted grace,
Time moves on, yet leaves no trace.

Stars arise, a twinkling sight,
Casting dreams in cold moonlight.
Each breath steams in the frigid air,
Subtle remnants, beauty rare.

Days grow longer, warmth will creep,
Yet in memory, winter's keep.
A frosty kiss, a fleeting thing,
Nature's dance as seasons sing.

## Veil of the Midnight Breeze

Silken sighs weave through the trees,
Carried gently on the midnight breeze.
Moonlight bathes the world in silver,
A quiet calm makes the heart quiver.

Stars wink softly from their throne,
In the stillness, we are alone.
Each rustle is a whispered tune,
A serenade to the watching moon.

Shadows play beneath the sky,
Dancing lightly, they flutter by.
Veils of silence, sweet allure,
In this moment, we are pure.

Breezes carry dreams untold,
Secrets whispered, soft and bold.
In the night, we lose our fears,
Embraced by the wind, through the years.

Stars reflect our hopes and schemes,
Glinting softly in our dreams.
As night deepens, hearts do seize,
Alive in the veil of midnight breeze.

## In the Absence of Sound

Silence enfolds like a whispered prayer,
Time stands still in the cool night air.
Thoughts unravel, flowing slow,
In the absence, life starts to grow.

Gentle echoes fade away,
Moments linger, a soft ballet.
Breath of peace calms the mind,
In quiet spaces, truth we find.

Shadows linger, light breaks free,
In the hush, we simply be.
Stars twinkle, a subtle spark,
Illuminating the profound dark.

Heartbeats become the music rare,
As stillness paints the evening air.
Each pulse echoes, soft and clear,
In absence of sound, we draw near.

Whispers of hope gently rise,
In embrace with the silent skies.
Finding solace, wrapped in peace,
In the absence, we find release.

**Crystalline Dreams**

Frosted visions dance in the night,
Crystalline forms, pure and bright.
Glistening like stars on the ground,
In silent beauty, secrets abound.

Sparkling fragments, shimmering light,
Whispers of magic take flight.
Each flake tells a story untold,
In their embrace, warmth unfolds.

Dreams float softly on winter's breath,
Carried through shadows, touched by death.
Yet in the cold, we find the spark,
Crystalline dreams, bright in the dark.

Glistening whispers of hopes deferred,
Every twinkle a heartfelt word.
Seasons change, yet dreams remain,
Crystalline visions, joy and pain.

We wander through the frosty air,
Seeking solace, unaware.
In the icy grasp, dreams are crowned,
Crystalline wonders, beauty profound.

## **Echoes of the Frostbitten Past**

In whispers low, the cold winds sigh,
As memories drift and quietly cry.
Footprints buried under snow's embrace,
Familiar faces lost without a trace.

Barren branches reach toward the gray,
Silent witnesses of disarray.
The heart remembers what time forgot,
A frozen dream in a frozen plot.

Echoes linger, haunting the dawn,
Where laughter once danced, now shadows yawn.
The chill settles in the bones of the night,
As the past unfolds in the pale moonlight.

Frost-kissed tales whisper from the trees,
Carried along on a bitter breeze.
The world is still, a canvas white,
Painting the echoes of lost delight.

So pause a moment, heed the sound,
Of frostbitten echoes all around.
In every flake, a memory cast,
Beneath the snow lies the faded past.

## Winter's Uneasy Soliloquy

The world holds its breath beneath the frost,
In every moment, a silence embossed.
Winter's voice carries, thick and slow,
A soliloquy where shadows grow.

Candles flicker against the chill,
Casting warmth, yet time stands still.
Thoughts wander like snowflakes that drift,
A fragile moment, a chilling gift.

Heartbeat echoes in the quiet night,
As dreams melt gently in fleeting light.
Each breath a vapor in the fray,
Winter speaks softly, then fades away.

Footprints mark the paths of the brave,
Seeking solace where the echoes wade.
The sun peeks shyly over the hills,
Awakening life with hesitant thrills.

A shroud of white clings to every tree,
As nature whispers, "Remember me."
Yet in the stillness, a hope will bloom,
A promise held within winter's gloom.

## The Veiled Dance of Shadows

Under the veil of the dim-lit night,
Shadows come alive, a spectral sight.
They waltz and whirl in a ghostly trance,
Each step revealing a forgotten dance.

The moonlight spills on the frosty ground,
Casting shapes where silence resounds.
Figures flicker, haunting the air,
Remnants of moments beyond compare.

In this masquerade, whispers take flight,
Echoing tales of forgotten light.
Each breath a story, a journey untold,
Held in the darkness, both timid and bold.

Stars twinkle softly, a watchful gaze,
As shadows perform in a mystical haze.
They linger, they twist, they blend with despair,
A testament of all that once lived there.

When dawn breaks softly, the dance will cease,
Yet in the heart, a sliver of peace.
For shadows may fade with the rise of day,
But their whispered secrets are here to stay.

## **Soft Murmurs in Winter's Embrace**

A hush pervades the crisp, cold air,
Whispers of winter, laden with care.
Snow blankets all in a gentle fold,
Soft murmurs echo, stories untold.

The trees stand sentinel, reaching high,
Clad in white, beneath the waning sky.
Each flake a note in a winter's song,
As time slips onward, where dreams belong.

Candlelit glow spills warm from within,
Guiding the way as twilight begins.
In every heartbeat, a rhythm subtle,
Carrying secrets, the winter's cuddle.

Through windows fogged with a breath's sigh,
We watch the world, where the wild winds cry.
Beneath the surface, life still survives,
Waiting for spring when the heart revives.

So cherish the moments, the whispers, the peace,
In winter's embrace, let your worries cease.
For in this stillness, we find our grace,
In soft murmurs held in winter's embrace.

## The Serenity of Frozen Landscapes


In stillness lies the glistening frost,
A canvas white, where dreams are lost.
Tall pines stand guard, serene and proud,
Whispers of peace drift soft, not loud.

Each crystal flake a fleeting friend,
In silence, winter's chill descends.
The world transformed, a pure embrace,
Nature's beauty, a quiet grace.

Both shadow and light in harmony blend,
Where earth and sky seem to extend.
Footprints mark paths of fleeting time,
In frozen realms, our spirits climb.

The air a breath of crisp delight,
Within the hush of winter's night.
Moonlight dances on drifts so high,
Ethereal sights that catch the eye.

Wrapped in white, the world shines bright,
Awakening hearts in soft twilight.
With every gust, a new refrain,
Serenity flows through joy and pain.

## The Sound of Softly Falling Snow

A gentle hush blankets the ground,
In whispers, soft snowflakes abound.
Each flake a tale from skies above,
Creating a world, a symphony of love.

Listen close to the quiet song,
As winter's breath lingers long.
The muffled sounds of day-to-day,
Fade into night, melt away.

Crystals shimmer in pale moonlight,
Transforming shadows, painting bright.
Nature's hush, a soothing balm,
Bringing peace, a quiet calm.

Frosty air dances with delight,
As snowflakes spiral out of sight.
Each landing brings a tender grace,
Soft whispers fill the empty space.

A world reborn in sparkling glow,
Suspended time in falling snow.
In this moment, hearts unite,
In the gentle touch of starry night.

## When Nature Holds Its Breath

In the stillness where silence reigns,
Time suspends, and peace remains.
Nature pauses, whispers low,
As if to say, 'Let wonder grow.'

Frozen lakes wear a crystal crown,
In waiting stillness, earth looks down.
The trees hold secrets, ancient, wise,
Veiled in mystery under skies.

Winter's chill brings a sacred space,
Where each heartbeat finds its place.
Around the trees, the shadows play,
In nature's pause, we drift away.

The breath of winter, crisp and clean,
Embraces all in tranquil sheen.
In distant hills, the echoes blend,
A symphony where moments bend.

And as the world holds its breath tight,
In this stillness, we find our light.
Awake in wonder, hearts expand,
In the embrace of this quiet land.

## **A World Wrapped in White**

A blanket soft as tender dreams,
The world adorns in twilight beams.
Whispers of snowflake lullabies,
Wrap the earth in sweet goodbyes.

Each flake a miracle of design,
A dance of beauty, every line.
The sun dips low, with rosy hues,
Painting the sky with gentle views.

Mountains stand tall in silent grace,
Guardians of this pristine place.
Through branches bare, the light will play,
In a world where shadows sway.

Footsteps crunch on this frosted land,
In the snow, we carve and stand.
The chill in air, a vibrant thrill,
In every breath, the quiet fills.

As night descends, a starry dome,
Each twinkling light, a distant home.
Wrapped in white, we pause, we stare,
In the magic woven everywhere.

## Ethereal Stillness

In the hush of fading light,
Stars awaken, soft and bright.
Whispers float on gentle breeze,
Carrying secrets through the trees.

Moonlight spills on dew-kissed grass,
Each moment fleeting, none shall last.
Shadows dance in silvered glow,
Nature's heart, a tranquil show.

Crickets sing their serenade,
In the calm, fears start to fade.
All is quiet, all is still,
Embraced by night, the world can heal.

Barefoot dreams on soft, cool ground,
In this peace, all hope is found.
Here we breathe, let worries cease,
Lost in time, we find our peace.

## **The Weight of a Quiet Evening**

The sun sinks low, a molten hue,
Colors blend in shades anew.
Breath of night, it starts to fall,
Echoes whisper, soft and small.

A distant train sings through the air,
Each note heavy with despair.
Moments linger, thick and sweet,
Time slows down, no heart to beat.

Stars emerge, one by one,
As the day gives way to none.
Shadows stretch, they twist and sway,
In this stillness, hopes decay.

Candles flicker, soft and bright,
Warding off encroaching night.
Thoughts are clouds, gentle, gray,
Sailing slowly, drift away.

In the quiet, burdens weigh,
Memories haunt like ghosts in play.
Yet here in dark, we find our way,
Guided by the stars' soft ray.

## Lonesome Landscapes under Gray Skies

Rolling hills in muted tones,
Where silence drapes like heavy loans.
Trees stand tall, yet seem to weep,
Secrets buried, dreams to keep.

Fields stretch wide, a barren sight,
The wind carries whispers of plight.
Clouds gather, a shroud of stone,
In this place, I stand alone.

Rivers flow in murky seams,
Reflections hold forgotten dreams.
Mountains loom like ancient tales,
Their wisdom lost in muted gales.

A hawk calls high, a sound so pure,
Yet in its cry, an ache for sure.
Each moment lingers, thick and gray,
In this vastness, I drift away.

Life moves slow in lonesome lands,
Where hope's light barely stands.
Beneath the weight of a heavy sky,
I search for reasons, ask why.

## Where the Chill Attempts to Speak

Breath mist forms in cold air's bite,
Nature shivers, cloaked in night.
A barren branch, stark and bare,
In the chill, whispers hang in air.

Frost weaves webs on windowpanes,
Each caress, a tale of pains.
The world is hushed, secrets seep,
Into shadows where shadows creep.

Footsteps crunch on frozen ground,
Echoes of my thoughts, profound.
Winter's grip, a harsh embrace,
Yet in the cold, I find my place.

Voices fade as night descends,
In the chill, the heart contends.
Under starlight, fears take flight,
Finding solace in the night.

Still the chill attempts to speak,
In its silence, wisdom seeks.
To hear the whispers, soft and clear,
Is to embrace what we hold dear.

## **Wistful Dreams in a Winter Grove**

In the grove where shadows play,
Wistful dreams softly sway,
Snowflakes whisper tales untold,
In the quiet, hearts unfold.

Beneath the boughs, the silence hums,
As winter's breath gently comes,
Footprints mark the path of time,
Echoes of a distant chime.

Frosty branches arch above,
A testament to fleeting love,
Memories entwined in white,
In the dawn's soft, golden light.

Chill of night in moonlit flight,
Guides the dreams to take their height,
Glowing softly, stars still gleam,
In the magic of a dream.

When the dawn begins to break,
Hearts awake, the echoes shake,
Winter's song fades with the day,
Yet in dreams, we'll find our way.

## **Glistening Silence**

In the twilight, whispers freeze,
Glistening silence in the trees,
Frosty breath adorns the air,
A stillness deep, beyond compare.

Crystals form on every bough,
Nature's art, a sacred vow,
Footsteps muffled by the snow,
In this hush, our spirits glow.

Moonlight dances on the ground,
Where hidden dreams can be found,
Shimmering under starlit gaze,
Time stands still in gentle haze.

Every flake tells tales of old,
Moments kept, and stories told,
In this glistening embrace of night,
The heart takes flight, pure and light.

Beyond the chill, a warmth resides,
In glistening silence, hope abides,
As dawn approaches, shadows fade,
In light's arrival, dreams are made.

## **Treading Softly on Glacial Ground**


On glacial ground, we move with grace,
Treading softly in this place,
Where ancient ice meets azure sky,
In the still, our spirits fly.

Each crackle and pop beneath our feet,
A symphony so bittersweet,
Nature's voice in whispers low,
Guiding us where few will go.

Frozen rivers, crystal clear,
Reflecting dreams that linger near,
Breath of winter fills the air,
A magic moment, rare and fair.

In this vast, white, silent sea,
We discover what it means to be,
Bound to earth, yet reaching far,
A fleeting glimpse of who we are.

With every step, a story grows,
In glacial winds, the heart still knows,
Where whispers of the past resound,
In the peace of glacial ground.

## A Breath on Frozen Glass

A breath on frozen glass inspires,
Misty sighs of muted fires,
In delicate frost, our marks remain,
A fleeting dance, a soft refrain.

Patterns swirl like dreams at play,
In winter's grasp, they drift away,
Each exhale forms a fleeting art,
A glimpse of warmth within the heart.

Glimmers caught in silent light,
Shimmering shards in the quiet night,
We trace our fingers, lost in thought,
In this stillness, solace sought.

Fleeting moments pressed in time,
Echoes of a gentle rhyme,
A breath upon each pane of glass,
A tender truth, as seasons pass.

When thaw arrives, and shadows fade,
Memories of winter's serenade,
In the warmth of spring, we find,
The breath of life, both soft and kind.

## **Whispers of the Frosty Moon**

In the night, the moon does glow,
Casting light on the fields below.
Whispers silver in the chill,
As time stands still upon the hill.

Frozen trees with branches bare,
Hold secrets whispered in the air.
The stars twinkle, a fleeting kiss,
In the stillness, find your bliss.

A blanket white covers the ground,
Where echoes of footsteps softly sound.
Moonbeams dance on frozen streams,
Awakening the world of dreams.

Each breath clouded in the night,
A gentle breeze, a soft delight.
Under frost, the shadows play,
Guided by the silver ray.

In the quiet, hearts embrace,
Finding solace in this space.
With the moon as our sweet guide,
In its light, we will abide.

## Shadows of the Quiet Meadow

In the meadow, shadows blend,
Where time and silence gently bend.
Beneath the sky, vast and wide,
Nature whispers, secrets hide.

Tall grasses dance in the breeze,
A soft rustle among the trees.
Colors fade as daylight wanes,
A soothing calm that still remains.

Crickets sing a lullaby,
As the sun begins to die.
Stars peek out, one by one,
The twilight beckons, day is done.

Fireflies twinkle, a fleeting spark,
Lighting up the stretching dark.
Each moment wrapped in the night,
Shadows cradle the fading light.

In this calm, our hearts align,
With nature's rhythm, pure, divine.
Together we shall find our place,
In the stillness, feel the grace.

## A Dance of Ice and Silence

In the heart of winter's chill,
Where ice encases every hill.
A quiet world, serene and bright,
Dances softly in the night.

Moonlight glimmers on the lake,
Reflecting dreams that gently wake.
Frosty whispers weave their spell,
In this place where magic dwells.

Footsteps crunch on powdered snow,
As shadows stretch and softly grow.
Each breath forms a fleeting mist,
In the hush, we simply exist.

Branches heavy, laden down,
Adorned in nature's crystal crown.
Silence reigns, profound and deep,
In this moment, memories keep.

The stillness sings a timeless song,
Echoing where we belong.
Together we embrace the cold,
In this dance, a story told.

## The Lullaby of Empty Streets

In the stillness of the town,
Beneath the stars, a gentle crown.
Empty streets, a silent call,
Where shadows stretch and softly fall.

Streetlights flicker, a soft glow,
Illuminating paths we know.
Whispers carried on the breeze,
The night wraps us in its ease.

Footsteps echo, soft and clear,
Each sound dissipates the fear.
In this space, the world is ours,
Underneath the watchful stars.

Windows dark, hearts alight,
In solitude, we find our might.
Dreams are woven, hope takes flight,
In the embrace of soft moonlight.

As we wander through the night,
The lullaby feels just right.
Empty streets, a peaceful song,
In their silence, we belong.

## **Lullabies of the Winter Wind**

Whispers soft through trees stand bare,
A soothing hymn, a tender care.
The frosty breath of night descends,
As nature's voice in silence wends.

Moonlight dances on the snow,
A gentle touch where shadows flow.
The world wrapped tight in icy dreams,
Unfolds in peace, or so it seems.

Stars twinkle in the velvet sky,
While winter sighs, a lullaby.
Embraced by chill, we find our peace,
In winter's hold, all worries cease.

Crisp are the nights, the days so bright,
Each breath a cloud, a fleeting sight.
The lullabies in breezes hum,
As time in stillness softly strums.

Close your eyes, let worries go,
In winter's arms, feel love's warm glow.
For in the night, the heart can mend,
To winter's song, we all descend.

## **Muffled Footfalls in White**

As snowflakes fall in quiet grace,
Footsteps fade, a gentle trace.
The world transformed, so soft, so bright,
In winter's hush, the heart takes flight.

Blankets woven, silver strands,
Covering all, nature's hands.
Whispers echo through the air,
A melody beyond compare.

Each step a dance, a soft embrace,
Crystals glitter with fine lace.
Muffled footfalls leave their mark,
In a canvas white and stark.

Trees adorned in frosty blooms,
Nature's breath in silent rooms.
The world a stage for dreams to play,
In winter's chill, we drift away.

Breathe in the air, so crisp, so pure,
In every heartbeat, feel secure.
Muffled memories wrap around,
In winter's arms, our joys abound.

## **Ghosts of the Frozen Breeze**

Through the cold, the shadows swing,
Ghosts of winter softly cling.
Echoes of a time once warm,
Now reside in autumn's charm.

Chill whispers tales of yesteryear,
In frozen breaths, old laughter near.
Flickers of warmth in memories fade,
Haunting dreams in twilight's shade.

The sky dressed in its grayest shroud,
While haunting winds weave through the crowd.
In search of light, we must persist,
With every chill, a velvet mist.

Boughs bow low with burdened snow,
A dance of shadows in starlit glow.
Ghostly figures, lost yet free,
Carving paths where we can't see.

In every breath, a fleeting sigh,
Waltzing with ghosts as they fly.
With each soft breeze, they disappear,
Yet linger close, forever near.

## The Stillness of Fading Light

As daylight wanes, the shadows grow,
In twilight's grasp, soft currents flow.
A hush descends, the world grows still,
In fading light, time begins to chill.

Whispers fade into the night,
Stars awaken, bringing light.
Each moment brief, a fleeting sigh,
As the sun sets, the crows fly high.

Colors blend, a painted sky,
With strokes of gold as day bids bye.
In stillness wrapped, the heart finds peace,
Embracing quiet, worries cease.

As shadows stretch and darkness falls,
The night's embrace, a soft enthrall.
The quiet hum of evening's song,
In fading light, where dreams belong.

With tender grace, the stars ignite,
Beacons shimmering through the night.
In every breath, the stillness flows,
Fading light, where the heart knows.

## **Bated Breath of a Winter's Night**

The moon hangs low in a velvet sky,
Whispers of frost in the biting air.
Stars blink gently, like a lover's sigh,
Awakening dreams that linger there.

Trees stand silent, cloaked in white,
Shadows dance in the soft glow of light.
Each breath I take is slow and measured,
In this stillness, winter's joy is treasured.

A crisp embrace of the night so pure,
Nature's canvas, serene and demure.
Footsteps crunch on the crunchy snow,
Carving memories, as the chill winds blow.

The world seems hushed, adorned in grace,
Each flake a tale of a timeless place.
A heartbeats rhythm, a soothing song,
In winter's arms, where I belong.

With every breath, the cold grows deep,
In silent corners, memories sleep.
This winter night, my pausing heart,
In bated breath, we're never apart.

## **Invisible Threads of Cold**

In the twilight, shadows stretch far,
Invisible threads weaving tales anew.
The chill descends like a forgotten scar,
Embracing the earth with a shivering view.

Frosted whispers call to the trees,
Branches shiver in the frigid breeze.
Nature holds secrets, wrapped in white,
Treasures hidden from the wandering sight.

Under the stars, a blanket of frost,
Each breath a vapor, a moment lost.
Night drapes softly in velvet shrouds,
As dreams drift forth in silent crowds.

The moon peers down with a watchful eye,
Lending light to the secrets that lie.
Each glimmering flake, a story untold,
In invisible threads of the winter's cold.

With every heartbeat, the chill sings low,
Drawing me into its quiet glow.
Wrapped in this magic, I find my peace,
In invisible threads, my worries cease.

# The Chilling Serenade of Solitude

In the heart of night, the chill unfolds,
A serenade sung by the wind's soft sigh.
With every gust, a secret told,
A melody echoes, beneath the sky.

Stars twinkle bright, like frozen tears,
Carving silence into gentle tones.
Each whisper of snow calms all my fears,
In solitude, my heart finds its home.

The world beyond feels distant, far,
Wrapped in layers of frost and peace.
Memory dances like a wandering star,
And with every note, all troubles cease.

As shadows stretch across the land,
In winter's grasp, I take my stand.
In the chilling song of the silent night,
I find my strength in the pale moonlight.

With every breath, the chill remains,
A soothing balm for past refrains.
In solitude's arms, my spirit grows,
In this serenade, true beauty flows.

## Fantasies of the Icy Realm

Deep in the heart of winter's embrace,
An icy realm awaits my gaze.
Crystal castles in a frosty space,
Sparkling dreams that fill the days.

Whispers of magic dance on the breeze,
Fantasies born from the snowflakes' flight.
Nature's wonders put my mind at ease,
In this frozen land, everything feels right.

The air, a canvas of glistening white,
Painting dreams in the softest hues.
Every corner alive, a shared delight,
I find solace in what winter imbues.

As night descends, the stars come alive,
Each one a promise, a spark in the dark.
Within this glory, my hopes revive,
In the enchantment of this icy park.

Fantasies dance on the crystalline floor,
A celebration of peace and grace.
In winter's hold, I long for more,
For in this realm, I've found my place.

## **Whispers in Frosted Air**

Soft whispers dance in the night,
A chill creeping through the air.
Frosted breath glimmers with light,
Nature's secrets laid bare.

Trees stand tall, cloaked in white,
Their branches dress in splendor.
Silent echoes take flight,
In whispers, the world surrenders.

Footsteps crunch on the ground,
Each one a tale to be told.
In solitude, joy is found,
A beauty that never grows old.

Stars twinkle in the vast sky,
A blanket of dreams once cast.
Beneath their gaze, spirits fly,
In moments that forever last.

The night deepens, shadows play,
In silence, hearts intertwine.
Whispers of love gently sway,
In frosted air, all is divine.

## Echoes of the Still Night

The stillness wraps around me tight,
Stars shimmer in the endless dark.
Whispers echo, soft and light,
Carrying tales from the heart.

Moonbeams cast a silver glow,
Painting dreams on the ground.
In this magic, time moves slow,
Each heartbeat is a profound sound.

Trees sway gently in the breeze,
A lullaby for slumbering souls.
Secrets mingling with the leaves,
Night's embrace makes us whole.

A distant hoot sings of the night,
Reminding me of moments passed.
Every breath feels so right,
In echoes that forever last.

Wrapped in peace, I close my eyes,
The world fades, and dreams take flight.
In this place where stillness lies,
I am free, embraced by night.

## The Quiet Embrace of Winter


Winter whispers with a sigh,
A gentle hush upon the earth.
Frosty kisses float on high,
In silence, a new rebirth.

Blankets of white cover the ground,
Softly muffling every sound.
In this quiet, peace is found,
Where stillness and dreams abound.

Time slows down, as moments pause,
In the arms of winter's grace.
Every flake, a nature's cause,
As beauty falls, we find our place.

Candles flicker, warm and bright,
Casting shadows on the walls.
In this embrace of chilly night,
Love's warm glow gently calls.

Hot cocoa warms our hands,
While stories dance in the air.
Together, through snowy lands,
We share the quiet we bear.

## Shadows Beneath the Moonlight

Shadows stretch across the floor,
Cradled by the moon's sweet beam.
In the stillness, spirits soar,
And reality turns to dream.

Night birds call with haunting grace,
As whispers linger on the breeze.
In this place, I find my space,
Where heart and soul feel at ease.

Moonbeams dance on the water's skin,
A mirror of the cosmos wide.
Ripples where the dreams begin,
In the silence, joy resides.

The forest breathes a mystic air,
As shadows weave their tapestry.
In this realm, devoid of care,
Nature speaks so fervently.

Each heartbeat echoes in the night,
With shadows gathered round the flame.
In the dark, we find our light,
No two moments are the same.

## **Pantomime of the Shivering Night**


The moon hangs low, a silver thread,
Whispers of frost dance in the air.
Shadows play where the lovers tread,
Under the night's soft, chilling glare.

Stars twinkle like eyes, so bright,
Watching the secrets unfold below.
A silent stage of pure delight,
As winter's breath begins to blow.

Branches sway with a ghostly grace,
Wrapped in a cloak of frosty white.
Nature weaves a delicate lace,
In the pantomime of shivering night.

Echoes of laughter drift away,
Lost in the arms of frosty winds.
Time pauses in the twilight play,
Where every heartbeat echoes, spins.

Beneath the stars, we softly sigh,
Caught in the web of wintry dreams.
With every glance, the night glides by,
In the silence, nothing's as it seems.

## Silent Footprints on the Frozen Path

Footprints leave a tale untold,
Etched in snow, a fleeting trace.
Whispers of stories, brave and bold,
On this path, we find our place.

Each step a heartbeat in the chill,
Silence wraps the world in peace.
From the mountain's edge, to the hill,
Nature's sighs never cease.

The night sky drapes a velvet well,
Stars sprinkle down their gentle light.
In the stillness, we hear the bell,
Of winter's calm, a serene sight.

Frozen branches, a crystal lace,
Crackle softly under the weight.
In this moment, we embrace,
The quiet beauty, simple fate.

Silent footprints guide our hearts,
On this path where dreams reside.
With every step, new magic starts,
As we walk, the world's our guide.

## The Quietude of Shivering Pines

In the forest, whispers flow,
Pines shiver in the crisp, cold air.
An ancient song, quiet and slow,
Crafts a melody of silent care.

Moonlight dapples through the leaves,
Creating shadows, soft and deep.
Where every branch the secret weaves,
In the stillness, nature keeps.

Echoes linger of nights gone by,
Dancing with the frost-kissed breeze.
While stars twinkle in the midnight sky,
Wandering lost among the trees.

The scent of pine, a calming balm,
Wraps around our weary minds.
In this haven, all is calm,
The quietude of time unwinds.

Moments freeze beneath the sky,
Where winter's breath paints every scene.
Together, you and I,
In the woods, we breathe serene.

## Riddles in the Winter Haze

A fog descends, thick as a dream,
Hiding secrets in its soft embrace.
Whispers linger, a haunting theme,
In the stillness of this frozen space.

Figures dance beneath the gray,
Each shadow a riddle, unknown.
The world is quiet, turned to clay,
As winter's magic turns to stone.

Snowflakes fall like silent tears,
Each one a question, pure and white.
In the chill, we face our fears,
Searching for answers in the night.

Branches twist in a curious form,
Carved by winds that twist and turn.
Nature's art, a breathless storm,
In the haze where our hearts yearn.

Riddles wrapped in winter's chill,
Call to us from deep within.
As we wander, let time stand still,
Finding warmth where dreams begin.

## **Breath of the Frozen Wind**

Whispers cut through the still air,
A chill dances on my skin.
Each gust tells a secret tale,
Of winter's heart deep within.

Snowflakes swirl in a fleeting blur,
Softly landing on frosted eaves.
Nature holds its breath, so pure,
In this realm where no one grieves.

Branches sway, their shadows long,
Echos of the silent night.
I hear the wind's forgotten song,
A moan of cold, a soft despite.

Inhale the icy twilight glow,
As stars peek through the blackened sky.
A canvas white, where dreams can flow,
In the realm where winter lies.

Wrapped in layers, I feel alive,
The frozen wind, it beckons near.
Here in the cold, my heart will thrive,
With each breath, I have no fear.

## **Hushed Impressions on the Ground**


Footsteps crunch on powdered snow,
Marking paths through dreams untold.
In silence, nature's wonders grow,
Each print a story, bright and bold.

A fleeting glance at the stars, they wink,
As shadows stretch and colors fade.
The earth, asleep, begins to think,
Of memories in the tranquil shade.

A whisper of trees, they nod and sway,
In the quiet, old tales unfold.
Every moment, night meets day,
In this dance of silver and gold.

With every step, a tale begins,
In the stillness, secrets found.
The world lies still, beneath my sins,
Hushed impressions on the ground.

As dawn paints the sky with pastel hues,
A canvas rich, with endless art.
In every shade, a soul renews,
And nature whispers to the heart.

## Unspoken Frost

Veils of frost, they shimmer bright,
Silent guardians of the night.
They cloak the world in icy grace,
A tranquil hush, a soft embrace.

Trees adorned like crystal crowns,
In the chill, they wear their gowns.
The moonlight glimmers on their skin,
A wintry dance that draws me in.

Each breath a cloud that fades away,
In this stillness, thoughts decay.
Nature's breath, a frozen plea,
Whispers lost in reverie.

A chilling kiss upon the ground,
Where beauty lies, yet not a sound.
In every flake, a dream confined,
Unspoken frost, where hearts unwind.

In the twilight, shadows play,
Swirling magic in their sway.
The world is hushed, a secret throng,
In winter's grasp, we all belong.

## When Icicles Listen

From rooftops high, they hang in grace,
Silent watchers, time's embrace.
Each droplet falls like whispered lore,
In the still air, a soft encore.

They glisten bright in morning's light,
A symphony of pure delight.
As shadows stretch and winter sighs,
The world beneath a canvas lies.

Old tales tell of frost and flame,
Of lovers' vows, of joy and pain.
When icicles listen, hearts awake,
In their stillness, dreams we make.

Nature waits for spring's caress,
In frozen time, we feel the press.
The magic lingers, light drifts in,
As new journeys prepare to begin.

With each shard's fall, a promise kept,
Of warmer days, where laughter leapt.
When icicles listen, whispers flow,
In the freeze, all love will grow.

**Frosted Frames of Time**


In the quiet hours of night,
Frozen whispers weave delight.
Moonlight dances on the glass,
Capturing moments as they pass.

Shadows flicker, gentle sighs,
Memories drift under starry skies.
Each breath steams in the chilly air,
Time stands still, a silent prayer.

Snowflakes fall like fragile dreams,
Layering silence in silver streams.
Every corner holds a tale,
History preserved, soft and pale.

Frosted edges, delicate frames,
Echoing softly forgotten names.
Through the glass, the past will show,
A tapestry of long-lost glow.

In this moment, time suspends,
Wrapped in beauty that never ends.
As dawn approaches, shadows flee,
Yet the memory remains with me.

## The Lonesome Chill of Dusk

Evening settles, cold and gray,
Whispers haunt the fading day.
A lonesome chill breathes through the trees,
Carrying secrets on the breeze.

Colors fade to muted tones,
Softly echoing twilight's groans.
The horizon glows, a flickering flame,
A world transformed, never the same.

Stars awaken, shy and small,
While shadows lengthen, begin to crawl.
In the distance, a lonely song,
Dusk cradles night where dreams belong.

Frosted breath, the air is tight,
Nights like this, the heart takes flight.
A journey waits beyond the veil,
In dusk's embrace, fears grow pale.

Under the shroud of quiet night,
Lies a shimmer, a diffused light.
With each heartbeat, the world stands still,
In the chill of dusk, time's gentle thrill.

## **Whispers of the Icy Void**

In the depths of an endless night,
Whispers echo, soft and slight.
Voices linger in frosted air,
Tales of the lost, beyond despair.

Frozen echoes, shadows play,
Drifting softly, far away.
The icy void, a haunting call,
Brings forth memories, one and all.

Each sigh carried on the breeze,
Songs played on the frozen trees.
A symphony of silent chords,
Unraveling truth as time rewards.

Constellations blink in sleepy skies,
Bearing witness to ancient ties.
The void whispers of days long gone,
In its embrace, we are all drawn.

Glacial beauty, still and profound,
Within the void, lost souls are found.
In the hush, we learn to be,
One with all, eternally free.

## **Xylophone Notes on Frigid Air**

Frosted xylophones play in the night,
Melodies dance in the pale moonlight.
Each note cascading, crystal clear,
Echoes ringing, the world draws near.

The chill breathes life into the sound,
Notes soaring high, none can be bound.
A harmony born of winter's chill,
Capturing hearts, a soft thrill.

Pine trees sway, keep time with grace,
Nature's rhythm, a delicate embrace.
The xylophone sings to the stars above,
A serenade of winter's love.

Each strike brings warmth to a frozen land,
A magic crafted by unseen hands.
At dawn's arrival, the song will fade,
Yet the essence of joy will never trade.

In the heart of winter's breath,
Lies a music that conquers death.
Xylophone whispers fill the air,
Fragrant with promise, beyond compare.

## Secrets in Crystal Silence

In the hush of night, shadows dance,
Whispers cling to the frosty air.
Crystals gleam, secrets held tight,
A world asleep, beyond compare.

Moonlight flickers on the stream,
Casting dreams in glimmers bright.
Nature's breath slows to a gleam,
Wrapped in silence, cloaked in light.

Beneath the stars, the silence sighs,
Each twinkle a hidden tale.
Echoes of all that once was wise,
In stillness, the universe prevails.

Hidden truths in slumber deep,
Crystals shimmer with myrrh's scent.
Guardians of the night, they keep,
Secrets of the night's content.

In the embrace of midnight's hold,
Time stands still, wrapped in white.
In crystal silence, stories unfold,
Whispers linger, pure delight.

## Tales of Cold Solitude

Winds howl through the barren trees,
A shiver runs down silent lanes.
Each breath clouds in the biting freeze,
Echoes of forgotten pains.

Footsteps crunch on frozen ground,
Loneliness paints the empty scene.
In the stillness, no one's found,
Just the cold, a haunting queen.

Snowflakes dance like memories lost,
Adrift in a vast and empty space.
In solitude, we count the cost,
Yearning for a warm embrace.

The horizon fades in muted gray,
A canvas blank, emotions stark.
Time drips slowly, day by day,
In solitude, we bear the mark.

Frozen hearts in winter's clasp,
Muffled dreams drift through the night.
In this tale, we find our grasp,
Cold solitude, with its own light.

## The Vast Desolation of Winter

Whispers of frost cling to the ground,
In the quiet void, nothing stays.
Nature sleeps, no soft sound,
In the grasp of winter's gaze.

Fields lie bare, a silver sheet,
Echoes fade in the frigid air.
A world so still, a distant beat,
Life subdued, lurking with care.

Mountains wear their icy crowns,
Crags and edges sharp and defined.
In this expanse, all joy drowns,
In desolation, warmth behind.

Yet wonder lies in bleakness found,
Beauty glimmers in every flake.
In dullness, life can still astound,
Through bitter dreams, new paths we make.

Winter's breath, a chilling song,
Harmonies of silence rove.
In the vastness where we belong,
Desolation hides the seeds of love.

## Moods Caked in Ice

Frozen thoughts in winter's grip,
Feelings trapped, yet striving free.
Each moment's a precarious trip,
Shadows of what used to be.

A heart encased in frosted tears,
Wrapped in layers of cold despair.
Echoes linger, feeding fears,
In the stillness, memories flare.

The chill creeps deep in every crack,
Brittle edges of love retain.
Desires sound a solitary clack,
In the freeze, we search for grain.

Yet in the ice, warmth hides its face,
Flickers of hope break through the night.
In this mood, we find our place,
Caked in ice, we dream of light.

Beneath the surface, life's pulse beats,
Waiting for thaw's gentle kiss.
In winter's hold, the heart still meets,
The promise of a brighter bliss.

# Chill's Gentle Touch

In the crisp air, whispers sigh,
Winter wraps the world so nigh.
Softly falling, flakes drift down,
A quiet blanket covers town.

Glistening light on branches bare,
Each breath hangs in frosty air.
Nature's hush, a tranquil spell,
In this chill, all is well.

Footsteps crunch on icy ground,
Echoes of peace all around.
The world slows in a serene dance,
Lost in winter's warm expanse.

Twilight falls, the colors fade,
Shadows stretch in evening's shade.
Stars emerge, twinkling bright,
Guiding hearts into the night.

As the cold seeps into bone,
In stillness, we've found our home.
Nature sleeps, we hold it dear,
In chill's embrace, we conquer fear.

## The Stillness Between Heartbeats

In quiet moments, time stands still,
Caught between each breath and will.
The space where silence softly breathes,
A tender pause, the heart believes.

Thoughts linger gently, like a sigh,
Watching as the moments fly.
In the hush, the world feels right,
As shadows stretch with fading light.

Here in twilight's gentle glow,
Feelings rise and ebb like flow.
A whisper shared without a sound,
In stillness, love is truly found.

The heartbeat echoes, strong and clear,
With every pulse, we draw near.
In the calm, we come to know,
The depth of silence, soft and slow.

As minutes wane and dusk descends,
In this pause, we find our friends.
In quietude, our spirits soar,
The stillness calls, forevermore.

## A Breath of Frozen Time

Frozen breath hangs in the air,
Moments captured, bright and rare.
Time stands still in winter's clutch,
Each heartbeat whispers of the touch.

Nature weaves a tapestry,
Of sparkling snow and majesty.
Underneath the silver light,
Dreams awaken in the night.

Stillness reigns, a calm embrace,
With winter's chill, we find our place.
A breath held tight, then softly released,
In frozen moments, joy's increased.

Branches bow with weighty grace,
Nature rests in this sacred space.
As the stars begin to gleam,
We find solace in the dream.

In each shimmer and every flake,
A new beginning starts to wake.
In this breath, our hearts align,
With every whisper, frozen time.

## **Frost-Laden Thoughts**

Frosted windows, visions blurred,
Whispers of the night unheard.
Thoughts like snowflakes softly fall,
Each one unique, a silent call.

In the chill, ideas bloom bright,
As winter's magic fills the night.
Quiet musings take their flight,
In frozen realms of pure delight.

Night wraps all in a tender shroud,
Thoughts drift high, soft and proud.
Crystals twinkle in the dark,
Each thought a fleeting, brilliant spark.

Beneath the frost, the world holds its breath,
Contemplating life, love, and death.
In the stillness, we find our way,
As dreams awaken with the day.

Frost-laden, the mind expands,
Painting visions with gentle hands.
In this chill, we learn to trust,
For in our thoughts, we find the dust.

## Hushed Moments at Dusk

The sun dips low, a golden shift,
Whispers of twilight begin to drift.
Silhouettes dance as shadows grow,
In this stillness, time moves slow.

Crickets sing their evening tune,
Under the watch of a crescent moon.
Stars awaken one by one,
Night enfolds what day has done.

A breeze carries secrets untold,
In twilight's arms, the world feels bold.
Dreams awaken from their sleep,
In quiet moments, silence deep.

Colors fade, yet beauty remains,
In every shadow, joy sustains.
Hushed moments cradle the day,
As darkness gently finds its way.

Nature whispers, soft and light,
Embraced by the softening night.
With every breath, time stands still,
In the dusk, there's a tranquil thrill.

## Where Silence Meets the Snow

Snowflakes dance upon the ground,
A hushed beauty all around.
Blankets white, so pure, so bright,
In silence, day turns into night.

Footsteps muffled, trails awash,
In this stillness, hearts do toss.
Winter's breath, a gentle sigh,
As clouds drift softly through the sky.

Trees wear coats of glistening white,
Branches whisper in fading light.
A world transformed, serene and slow,
Where silence meets the falling snow.

Cotton dreams drift from high above,
In this moment, we feel love.
Nature's lullaby, so soft, so low,
Tranquil beauty wrapped in snow.

Every flake, a story spun,
In winter's grasp, we become one.
With every breath, we find our way,
In the silence, we wish to stay.

## Veil of the Sombre Sky

Clouds gather thick, a muted gray,
Casting shadows on the day.
The air is heavy with whispered dread,
Beneath the veil where light has fled.

Raindrops tremble on windowpanes,
As nature keeps her soft refrains.
A symphony of sighs and moans,
In the stillness, we hear the tones.

Chill settles in, a sullen embrace,
We search for warmth in the empty space.
Branches sway in a ghostly dance,
Under the sky's melancholic glance.

Glimmers of light barely break through,
A promise of joy in a world so blue.
Yet in this gloom, there's beauty to find,
In the tender ties that life has twined.

Moments linger, wrapped in gray,
As we wander through the fray.
The sombre sky, a canvas wide,
Reminds us of the joy inside.

## Beneath the Blanketing Cold

Winter descends, a quiet shroud,
Nature's breath, a frosty cloud.
Underneath, the world lies still,
Embraced by snow on every hill.

The air is crisp, a piercing bite,
As stars twinkle in the velvet night.
The moon glows bright, casting its fold,
Beneath the blanketing cold.

Footprints tell stories in the white,
Echoes of laughter, hearts take flight.
Children play in the frosty glow,
Building dreams with each soft throw.

The world is hushed, the night is long,
In this stillness, we grow strong.
Under the blanket, warmth does unfold,
As we gather close from the chill and cold.

Whispers of night dance soft and low,
In the quiet, our spirits grow.
The beauty of winter, a tale retold,
Beneath the blanketing cold.

## Subtle Shivers

In the twilight's gentle breath,
Whispers dance on frozen air.
Underneath the waning light,
Shadows stretch without a care.

Leaves tremble in the night's embrace,
Moonlit secrets softly weave.
Heartbeats echo, lost in time,
Yearning sighs as dreams believe.

Stars twinkle in the velvet sky,
Each a wish, a silent plea.
Every shiver tells a tale,
Of longing set forever free.

Breezes tease with tender grace,
Lifting spirits from the ground.
In the stillness, we find peace,
In the quiet, love is found.

So we wander, hand in hand,
Through the whispers of the night.
In the dark, we find our way,
Guided by the distant light.

**Crystalline Dreams**

In the world of shimmering light,
Frozen wonders come alive.
Each glint and flicker tells a tale,
Of innocence and hopes that strive.

Reflections dance on icy ponds,
Glistening like the stars above.
With every breath, a crystal sigh,
Echoes of a tender love.

Through the frost, our footsteps trace,
Patterns only we can see.
In this chill, we find our warmth,
Wrapped in sweet simplicity.

Dreams entwined like fleeting smoke,
Woven into the night's embrace.
In the hush, we find our way,
Guided by the dreams we chase.

So let us wander through this realm,
Where crystalline visions gleam.
In every breath, a promise holds,
Life itself, a wondrous dream.

## **Frost-kissed Loneliness**

In the silence of the snow,
Words unspoken hang in air.
Loneliness wraps its chilly arms,
A shroud of beauty, stark and rare.

Footprints fading in the frost,
Tracing paths of those once near.
Shadows linger in the dusk,
Memories held close, yet unclear.

Winter's breath brings icy tears,
As moonlight bathes the world in white.
Through the chilly winds, I crave,
A gentle touch, a spark of light.

From the hollows of the heart,
Yearnings rise like smoke and mist.
Frost-kissed solitude holds sway,
In the quiet, love persists.

Yet in this frozen landscape wide,
Hope emerges, bright and bold.
For even in the coldest nights,
Warmth is found in stories told.

## Shadows beneath the Ice

Beneath the surface, whispers sigh,
Secrets trapped in crystal still.
Ghostly forms, they linger low,
Yearning for the world's warm thrill.

Darkness gathers on the edge,
Where sunlight barely dares to go.
In the depths, a world unknown,
Echoes of a time below.

Frozen tears and silent cries,
Echo through the depths of night.
In stillness, stories weave their path,
Shadows whisper, take to flight.

Yet every shadow bears its light,
In the heart of icy streams.
Within each stillness, life persists,
Woven into woven dreams.

So let us peek beneath the ice,
Discover what the cold conceals.
In the shadows, truths emerge,
Life continues, and love heals.

## The Hidden Lull of the Hearth

In ember's glow, the shadows sway,
Whispers of warmth, peace at bay.
Soft crackles hum a gentle tune,
Timeless stories beneath the moon.

Blankets wrapped, in dreams we roam,
The hearth holds secrets, calls us home.
Outside the chill, within our bliss,
A hidden lull, a tender kiss.

Flickering lights dance on the walls,
In this embrace, the silence falls.
Memories linger in the air,
Each moment treasured, none to spare.

The fire flickers, a lullaby,
As stars peek through the night sky high.
Embracing the warmth, we close our eyes,
The heart of the hearth, where love never dies.

With every spark, a wish ignites,
In the hidden lull, the spirit delights.
Together we find our souls' retreat,
In the hearth's warmth, our hearts will meet.

## When the Air Shivers

Beneath the trees, the whispers call,
As daylight fades, shadows enthrall.
A chill runs deep, the world holds breath,
In nature's pause, the dance of death.

Frosted leaves cling in sunlight's sigh,
The brisk embrace, an echoing cry.
Stars awaken, the night's serene,
In a hushed world, the unseen.

The stillness weaves a tapestry bright,
Of dreams that flitter in fading light.
Through biting winds, the spirits roam,
In the air's chill, they find their home.

Whispers of winter in every space,
Nature's fingers trace each face.
When the air shivers, hearts know the song,
In this embrace, we all belong.

As twilight dances, shadows blend,
A symphony played that will never end.
Cloaked in silence, we stand anew,
When the air shivers, the world feels true.

## **Resonance of the Icy Veil**

A tapestry spun of crystal grace,
Each flake a story, time won't erase.
The icy veil, a cloak of dreams,
Hides secrets whispered in moonlit beams.

In frost-laden branches, echoes wait,
Calling the dawn, it's never too late.
Silence reigns beneath the snow,
In the icy grip, new wonders grow.

Footsteps crunch on the frozen ground,
Amidst the stillness, beauty is found.
Nature's breath, a sigh so pure,
In the icy veil, hearts find a cure.

Beneath the layers, life holds tight,
Through every winter, follows the light.
Resonance echoes, a timeless dance,
In the frozen hush, we find our chance.

As the sun breaks through, the veil will lift,
Revealing the warmth, nature's gift.
In every shimmer, hope shall prevail,
A world reborn, through the icy veil.

## The Starkness of Solitude

In empty rooms, the silence sings,
A cry for warmth, a weight that clings.
Each shadow dances, a fleeting ghost,
In the starkness, we seek the most.

Walls echo whispers of days gone by,
Memories linger, the heart does sigh.
Alone yet whole, we learn to see,
In solitude's grasp, we find the key.

The clock ticks slowly, time stands still,
A canvas waiting, a cup to fill.
In deep reflection, the soul takes flight,
Unraveling dreams in the velvet night.

Through the starkness, a spark ignites,
Fleeting hopes like distant lights.
In the quiet, we mend our seams,
Crafting a world from scattered dreams.

With every heartbeat, solitude grows,
A garden nurtured by the self it sows.
In the echo of silence, we learn to be,
Finding our voice, setting it free.

Milton Keynes UK
Ingram Content Group UK Ltd.
UKHW010228111224
452348UK00011B/595